Ballroom Dance Class

Anton Du Beke

To my brother Stephen, my sister Veronica, and mostly
my Mum – without her what would I be?

I would like to thank all the teachers who've given me lessons: amongst many, Beryl and Velda Holton, Bill
and Sylvia Mitchell, Bob and Barbara Grover, Michael and Lorna Stylianos, Richard and Janet Gleave, Anne
Gleave, Michael and Vicky Barr, Anthony Hurley, Marcus and Karen Hilton, and John Del-roy.

Caroline Feraday and Sophie Allen helped me get the words onto the page. Louise keeps me out of trouble
and tries to get me there on time; without her I'd be nothing. Thanks too to Greg for his fabulous pictures,
David for depicting us in art. Geoff for his designs. Flavia for her body and Erin –
I am only half a man without Erin.

Thanks to Tony Brackley for the suits, Supadance for the shoes, DSI for the frocks – you're good to
Erin and me. And to my friends Stuart Rach and of course, Jeff.

Anton Du Beke

This edition first published in 2008
by Hinkler Books Pty Ltd
45–55 Fairchild Street
Heatherton Victoria 3202 Australia
www.hinklerbooks.com

First published in Great Britain in 2007
by Kyle Cathie Limited

Floral ornament © mehmet ali cida/istockphoto.com

Printed and bound in China

6 8 10 9 7 5
11 13 12 10

ISBN 978 1 7418 2565 7

Contents

Introduction

Welcome to my Ballroom dance class. Now this book is going to be a gentle introduction to Ballroom and Latin American dancing where we are going to have some fun without getting too bogged down in the technical jargon, but also give ourselves the sense of how it feels to dance because that great feeling of exhilaration that comes with moving across the floor in total harmony with your partner and spinning, turning, twirling, jiving is the most important thing. If you want high-level technique, go and have a lesson at a dance studio but, if you want to get a sense of how to dance and feel fabulous with it, read on. Hopefully this book will give you the confidence to join a local dance class and take your dancing to the next level. Dancing is a wonderful way of socialising, keeping fit and enjoying yourself.

Now, good dancing requires a few basic fundamentals. Here are the bits to think about time and again when you're getting in the mood to dance.

Posture
Posture is vitally important because the better the posture, the better the dancing; it is so much easier to dance with good posture. Bad posture leads to many problems – you'll be kicking each other half to death and won't be speaking by the end of the night. Good posture helps balance, the leading, the following and the transferring of weight – the overall movement. So, how do we stand? When you lift your arms into dance position make sure you don't lift your shoulders too. Boys first, stand with your feet together and standing tall, make sure your head, shoulders, chest and hips are lined up over each other over the centre of the foot and with your ribcage lifted and your arms hanging down by your side. Ladies, do the same thing. At this point, ladies, you might feel like you're sticking your chest out, but you're not, you're just standing correctly. There's something we call sunken chest syndrome; pick up your ribcage because it releases your hips and don't try to 'hide' your chest. Posture for the ladies is not to be confused with poise – we will come to that in a minute. And when you're dancing around the floor try to maintain your perfect posture. A quick word of advice for the boys: ladies like a man who stands tall, which makes him look elegant and refined, even if he's not in real life. You get a much better feel for the dance with good posture. New dancers particularly feel uncomfortable by the invasion of their space, more so with Latin American, but this can be helped by good posture too.

Poise
The poise of the body will add to the look and the balance of your dancing. For the ladies, in Ballroom, the poise is a slight curve to your left, with your head turned very slightly so that you can look over your wrist to the left but with your head continuing the line of your spine. For the

boys, the body should be leaning slightly forward. It's also important for boys and girls not to allow the weight of the body to be rocked onto the heels – always feel like you are on the middle to the front of your foot. In Latin American dancing, the body should be poised very slightly forwards for both boy and girl.

Footwork

This just describes the way you step onto different parts of your foot during individual steps. There are four parts of the foot used in great Ballroom and Latin dancing – toe, ball of the foot, flat foot (whole of it) and the heel. Never try to put your weight onto the outside edge of the foot until you're a professional dancer.

Rise and Fall

This interprets musicality and goes a little bit hand-in-glove with footwork, and describes elevation created by the straightening of the legs; when I rise onto my toes, I start to straighten my leg and stretch my body. Every Ballroom dance apart from Tango has the need for rise and fall – and I have described it in some detail in the exercise for the Waltz on pages 11–28.

Weight

It is true to say that when travelling forwards the weight of the body should be forwards, when travelling sideways, the weight of the body should be forwards, when travelling backwards, the weight

of the body should be … forwards. I think you could say there is a pattern forming. We are going to discuss the transferring of weight a lot in this book because when people learn to dance they learn to fully transfer weight properly. The weight of the body should fully transfer from one foot to the other; at no time should the weight be split between the two feet. The elegance of dancing comes from having the weight on only one foot at a time and truly transferring the whole body weight with each step.

Balance

When you move forwards or backwards, good balance makes for elegance and ease of movement; it is probably the most important element of making you a good dancer. It means that the carriage of your weight is in the right place. It means that your body can move freely and your legs can swing freely from the hips. Think about it as you learn and relax along the way.

The Hold

How do you hold? Boys, we're getting to the good bit now, this is where you're allowed to touch your partner but you've got to do it nicely, otherwise the ladies will talk about you in the powder room. In the Ballroom hold, stand with the feet slightly apart, boys start off by raising the left arm so that the hand is slightly above the level of the shoulder, with the elbow slightly bent. The right hand should be placed just on or below the lady's left shoulder blade with the man's right elbow picked up to match the height of his left elbow without, of course, lifting the shoulders. It makes for a much better line and makes you look like you know what you're doing, which helps.

Now ladies, you raise your right arm up, placing your right hand in the man's left hand, palm to palm, slightly bending your right elbow. Then you place your left hand on the man's upper right arm, below his shoulder. Stand in front of your partner in a slightly offset position with your right fronts facing each other (i.e. slightly to the right side of the man). The normal hold in Latin American dancing is exactly the same hold but you stand about a foot apart (rather than the bodies touching).

Hands and Arms and Feet

When you are not holding your partner, use your hands and arms in such a way you don't look like an octopus falling out of a tree. Hold them out, extended all the way to the fingertips. The arms don't finish at the wrist, they finish at the fingertips, which completes the line. There has to be a softness but without them being floppy, so with tone.

Finish off the line of your body through your feet – particularly important in Latin. In Ballroom, go away and practise your walk – we're not flipper feet, we're dancing gods!

The Walk

The perfect walk is what we are trying to achieve. Now I appreciate that when you walk down the street you won't walk like this, so let's be realistic and start with the getting to the bus walk and we can work up to the Anton Walk. But if you get this walk perfected, think how fabulously you will be able to dance.

Through each of the dances I've incorporated an exercise. Some of the exercises are basic figures that I believe develop the whole feeling of the dance and others are just the walk, which we've highlighted in greater detail below. Whatever they are, they are good exercise too. The great thing about the walk is that it incorporates all the points that we need to keep thinking about – posture, transference of weight and timing are the key elements – and if you can perfect these basics then you will get the feeling of being a dancer. One of the great joys of dancing is to *feel* the dancing. And you don't have to be a great dancer to feel great dancing.

The walk is a major part of Ballroom dancing and begins with the feet closed and the weight equally balanced, with the knees slightly flexed. The body starts to move first, the man stepping forward with the ball of the moving foot skimming the floor, going onto the heel at the same time that the heel of the supporting foot releases. The weight is now central on both feet and I call this the Johnny Walker moment – on the heel of the front foot and the ball of the back foot, passing through as the front foot goes flat taking the weight of the body, the back foot is pulled up from the toe, then ball of foot, going flat as it passes the standing foot. Ladies, remember that the man is leading and in control, and you are moving as one.

Now the backward walk starts again with the feet together, knees slightly flexed and weight equally apportioned. The leg swinging backwards from the hip extends to the toe, then moves onto the ball, with the weight of the body remaining on the front foot. As you start to transfer the weight, the weight rolls from the toe of the back foot onto the ball, and at the same time releases the toe and the ball of the front foot; at this stage the knee of the front leg will be straight and the back knee somewhat flexed. The weight is now passing through central position with the weight on both the heel of the front foot and the ball of the back foot. Continuing, the heel of the front foot is lightly drawn towards the back foot skimming across the floor, whilst the heel of the back foot only lowers when the front foot (which is now flat) passes underneath you.

Alignment and Direction
This is about the feet and which way they are travelling and the alignment also relates

to the way you are facing in the room at the end of the step. The diagram shows you the basics; it can get more complicated for experienced dancers but this will get you off the starting blocks and covers the dance steps in this book.

1: Facing diagonally to centre
2: Facing line of dance
3: Facing diagonally to wall
4: Facing centre
5: Facing wall

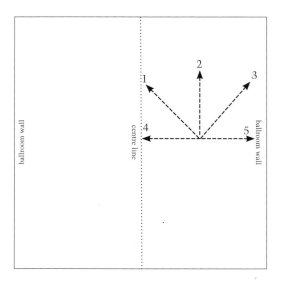

Leading and Following

I was once told that a good man follows what he leads, so boys, not only do you have to lead but you have to follow as well. There's a correct time to lead and an incorrect time to lead. The correct time is when you're taking a step: so, take a step and go from there. Once contact between partners is made, leading is through moving the hand to direct her to move as you will. Leading is a whole body experience – you can't just use one bit of your body – your leg or your hips, you've got to use everything. So, as you're taking a step and you want to turn to the right, for example, you take a step forward with your right foot and you must turn your whole body as well, indicating to the lady that you want to turn that way. I know it sounds like a simple thing but unless you turn everything you will find the message won't get across and you'll kick her, you'll run into her, she won't turn the correct way, simply because you are not leading properly. Now, ladies, what you have to do is pay attention to the lead, not anticipate or guess too much because he might change his mind.

Music

You may hear different things about music in Ballroom dancing. It is strict tempo because the speed of the music remains consistent throughout the dance. There is also time signature – how many beats and bars there are in a piece of music, for example in the Waltz it is 3/4 time, that's to say there are 3 beats in each bar of music. The Foxtrot and Quickstep are in 4/4 time, so there are 4 beats in each bar of music but, although they both have 4 beats in a bar, you cannot use the same piece of music because the tempos are different, with the Quickstep being almost double the speed. And the same goes for the Latin dances. The Cha Cha Cha and the Rumba are both in 4/4 time but the Rumba is much slower in tempo. Ballroom begins on the first beat in the bar, whereas, in the true spirit of Latin dances, it begins on the second beat of the bar.

Tempo

At its simplest, tempo is the speed at which the music is played or the number of bars per minute. The Viennese Waltz has around 52 bars to the minute whereas the Waltz has only 32 bars to the minute. Now, some bands play faster than others and, as a rule of thumb, for those that play faster than average, you should shorten the steps proportionately and, for those playing slower, then you should lengthen the steps appropriately.

Rhythm

The rhythm of the music refers to the recurring and accentuated beats and the length of the individual musical notes. It can also refer to whether you're dancing in time with the music or not, as the case may be! It's what gives dance life, colour and soul for me.

Ballroom and Latin American

The biggest difference with Ballroom and Latin dancing is the proximity, which seems bizarre because in Latin you are further apart. But the similarities are many – you still need to have good posture, great balance, transfer your weight, be in good time, lead your partner well, follow well – but the major difference is the hold. Sometimes you let go of each other altogether.

There is usually more of a narrative in the Latin dances and Rumba is the dance of love; Ballroom is more about motion and the movement of the dance than the suggestion of the choreography. There is a formality to the Ballroom dances, with the style of the dress and the fact that you don't actually look at each other. In Ballroom, there is a sense of one body, moving together in harmony, with the man moving for the lady. The movement, pattern and flow of the steps gives it the musicality and beauty. In Latin, the bodies move together but not in such harmonious unity, and there's more of a story. There is more interaction between boy and girl in the Latin dances – you get to look at each other.

How to Construct Dances

The construction of dances is like learning a language – the more words you learn, the better your vocabulary is, and dancing is exactly the same – the more steps you master the better and more developed the dance routine will be. You have to develop your vocabulary i.e. the steps, and then away you go from there. You are limited by the foot you have available as to what you can do.

So, in Ballroom, if you have your right foot available you will be turning invariably to the right, and if you have your left foot available you will be turning invariably to the left; sounds obvious, I know, but there will not be a time when you step forward on your right foot and turn to the left. And the same applies for the Latin.

For each of the dances I have given you a routine of steps to get you going. You'll find these on the first step of each of the dances.

Here are a couple of terms that will appear throughout the book that I think you should definitely come to grips with right at the beginning.

Promenade Position

The boy's right side and lady's left side are in contact at the ribcage level with the opposite sides of the body turned out to form a V. In Latin, it's exactly the same apart from the fact that the bodies are not in contact, just joined by the hands, but only facing each other with the opposite sides still turned out to form a V.

In Line

To step between your partner's feet, for the man and the lady.

Outside Partner

To step to the side of your partner's feet, not in line. I have always had a philosophy in dancing that the best way to improve quickly is not to dance with the same dancer all the time, so the best thing to do is ask other people to dance. So chaps, when you get the opportunity, take it.

Line of Dance

Once you've got dancing, you've taken hold, you've started to walk, you've got some music, you now need to know where to go, you need some direction – what we call the line of dance. The line of dance is very important because it's the direction in which we move around the floor. Some dances are slightly more stationary – the Jive and the Cha Cha Cha – but in the progressive dances, including all the Ballroom dances, you need to move anti-clockwise around the floor, because you never move around the floor against the line of dance – it would be like going up a one-way street the wrong way.

The Waltz

You probably don't expect to hear a Ballroom dance compared to an underwear drawer, but the Waltz is just that. It really *is* like your underwear drawer – you can just throw everything in! Choreography-wise I mean. The Waltz is a *big* dance – big turns, spins, great big sways and over sways. It's an opportunity to really experiment and to develop figures and timings, yet the elegant foundations of the dance remain throughout.

However, the Waltz doesn't start out as that and, as with so much, you have to start out at the beginning. Learning to dance the Waltz can feel somewhat slow and old-fashioned when you're learning and you can end up feeling as though you're not doing very much. Have you ever watched The Muppets? Animal is the mad drummer in the Muppets. Think of how he waves his arms around and hits all the drums and cymbals. However, in order to get to be the mad drummer, at the start he'd have to sit there with one drum, one stick – just going tap-tap-tap. It takes time and patience to get to be an 'Animal' on the drums. And the same is true of learning to be an animal dancing the Waltz.

I'll try to make it as much fun as possible and I can assure you that it's worth the patience and perseverance needed.

When I started to dance the Waltz I enjoyed it first of all, but went through a real phase of thinking that I couldn't stand it! Before too long I discovered how much there is to get out of dancing the Waltz. As I mentioned earlier, there's just so many different things which you can do and it's really worthwhile starting the journey. However, bear in mind that you do need to start off slowly and build up to the big, swinging swaying movements.

The Waltz is steeped in tradition, but you'll find that it doesn't feel old-fashioned. While it's the original Ballroom dance, and full of grace and elegance, it's a dance that's classical yet modern. So persevere with that tap-tap-tap with one stick on the drums and soon you'll be unleashed!

Here's an exercise to get you into the feel of dancing the Waltz. It's just three little steps – how hard could it be? Clearly, that's just a rhetorical question!

Firstly, starting off, let me remind you about posture and body position. Stand in front of your partner, with your bodies touching right front to right front. Take hold in the normal Ballroom position (see pages 6–7).

Now, here's what I want you to do. For the men, you're stepping forward with your right foot; it's just a straight step, by the way. Exactly the same as you take everyday – the same step you took when you walked into a shop and bought this book (thank you!). At the same time, ladies, I'd like you to step backwards with your left foot. Simple, eh?

So the man's weight is on his right foot, and the lady's is on her left foot. For the next step you're going to step to the side. So men, step to the side with your left foot. Ladies, you are stepping to the side with your right foot. At the same time you're transferring your weight onto that foot.

For the third step, you're closing your feet. So boys, close your right foot to your left and girls you're closing your left foot onto your right. It takes you back to the starting position. Three steps over three beats. I told you that it was easy.

Now, all you need to do is repeat this. The boys will start by putting their left foot forward this time and the girls will start with their right foot going back. So a simple step for beat one. Then take a step to the side for beat two, that's boys stepping with their right foot and girls with their left. For the third beat you're closing the step, so that's left foot to right foot for the boys and right foot to left foot if you're a girl. Again, you're back to where you started. Now, you're ready to use the right foot for the boy and left foot for the girl.

The most important part to remember with the steps here is never to use the same foot twice. You're always transferring weight

and then using the other foot. It sounds obvious when you say it, but it is harder to put into practice. Just remember that it's like walking – you don't use the same foot twice when you walk and nor do you when you waltz. When I'm teaching dancing – I'll always start people off on this exercise. Unless you can change weight correctly from one foot to the other in this exercise, I'm afraid the Waltz will be impossible.

In my experience, the biggest problem that people encounter is starting off with the same foot twice in a row. I don't know why this is, but it seems that it's so easy to forget which foot has just been used at the end of step three. The memory of which foot it was is wiped in an instant! So just try to keep in mind this rule about not using the same foot twice. You should be able to cheat your memory slightly and keep on track of the correct feet by slightly lifting the heel of the foot which you're about to use at the end of step three. Then you'll notice that it feels ready to use when you're finishing up that third step and ready to take step one again.

Now, one major characteristic of the Waltz, which we need to talk about is the rise and fall. Rise and fall certainly isn't unique to the Waltz. However, it's the rise and fall in this dance which gives it elegance. Forgive me if you already know about rise and fall but, even if you think that you do, it never hurts to refresh your memory. Perhaps you know about rise and fall from the other Ballroom dances, which they all have? Bear in mind that it is far more pronounced in the Waltz than with the others because of the closing of the feet in step three – which you did in our earlier exercise.

The Waltz

Rise and fall isn't about the steps – it's about the footwork. Have a think about how you normally use your feet when you walk. You would start on your heel and then go onto the flat of your foot when taking a step. That's a simple walking action. Now, the girls are going backwards – again thinking of the simple walking action – although walking backwards. Your foot would start on your toe and then go back onto the flat of your foot, wouldn't it? The Waltz is based on a walking action.

Now, let's do the exercise we did above but now start to think about the rise and fall. The first step is the same as when you walk, going from heel to flat foot – or toe to flat foot if you're going backwards. Then for the second step, the step to the side, you step to your toe and stay lifted up on your toe. So when you close the step by bringing your feet together you will have both feet on their toes with your heels off the ground. At the very end, you lower back down again and start all over. Now, the closing up and the lowering are both on beat three. You don't stay up, you move yourself up and then lower immediately. It may sound rather bizarre and complicated but it's really quite natural when you actually do it.

Now, you have the exercise we did earlier and I want you to do it, simply walking up and down the floor. Firstly all the way up, and then on the way back the boys will have to go backwards. Then I'd like you to repeat it, but adding in that rise and fall. And before you know it you'll be just like Animal from the Muppets! (That's a compliment, I promise!)

The music for a Waltz has a slow and somewhat melancholic feel and that's because of the timing. It's 3/4 time, which is three even beats to a bar. I've always thought that even the word Waltz conjurers up a picture of something rather old-fashioned, don't you agree? The melancholic music fits right into this for me – think about how something like 'Moon River' by Danny Williams has that feel, rather than a brighter 4/4 time piece of music. Now, don't assume that just because a piece of music is melancholic that it will fit the Waltz, it does have to be the more unusual 3/4 timing – as there are only three steps, and there are many pieces of slow music in 4/4 or other timings.

Natural turn

The Natural Turn is so called because it turns to the right; any turn to the left is called a reverse turning variation. Commence facing diagonally to the wall and end diagonally to the centre.

STEP 1

Man Step forward right foot

STEP 2

Man Step to the side left foot, turning right

STEP 3

Man Close right foot to left foot

Lady Step backwards left foot, turning right

Lady Step to the side right foot

Lady Close left foot to right foot

The Waltz

> ## Ideas for a basic dance sequence
> *Natural Turn, Change Step, Reverse Turn, Whisk into a Chassé*

STEP 4

Man Step backwards left foot, turning to the right

STEP 5

Man Step to the side right foot (shown here without turn, to show foot position)

STEP 6

Man Close left foot to right foot

Lady Step forward right foot, turning to the right

Lady Step to the side left foot, still turning to the right (shown here without turn, to show foot position)

Lady Close right foot to left foot

Reverse turn

Commence the Reverse Turn facing diagonally to centre and end facing diagonally to the wall. This step can be followed by a Whisk and a Chassé.

STEP 1

Man Step forward left foot, turning left

STEP 2

Man Step to the side right foot, still turning

STEP 3

Man Close left foot to right foot

Lady Step backwards right foot, turning left

Lady Step to the side left foot

Lady Close right foot to left foot

The Waltz

STEP 4

Man Step backwards right foot, turning left

STEP 5

Man Step to the side left foot (shown here without turn, to show foot position)

STEP 6

Man Close right foot to left foot

Lady Step forward left foot, turning left

Lady Step to the side right foot, still turning to the left (shown here without turn, to show foot position)

Lady Close left foot to right foot

Whisk

The Whisk can be followed by a Chassé. It is normally danced facing the wall.

STEP 1

Man Step forward left foot

Lady Step backwards right foot

The Waltz

STEP 2

Man Step to the side right foot

Lady Step to the side left foot

STEP 3

Man Cross left foot behind right foot, opening partner into Promenade Position

Lady Cross right foot behind left foot, turning into Promenade Position

Chassé

The Chassé is normally danced from a Whisk but it can be danced from any figure that ends in the Promenade Position.

STEP 1

Man Step forward right foot in Promenade Position

STEP 2

Man Step to the side and slightly forward left foot

Lady Step forward left foot, in Promenade Position

Lady Step to the side right foot, starting to turn to face partner

The Waltz

STEP 3

Man Close right foot to left foot

STEP 4

Man Step to the side and slightly forward left foot, preparing to step outside partner

Lady Close left foot to right foot, facing partner

Lady Step to the side right foot

Spin turn

The Spin Turn has a pivoting action for the man and a brushing action for the lady. It commences with the first three steps of a Natural Turn.

STEP 1

Man Step backwards left foot, pivoting on it to the right (keeping right foot in front of you)

Lady Step forward right foot, pivoting on it to the right

The Waltz

STEP 2

Man Step forward right foot, still turning to the right

Lady Step backwards left foot, still turning, and brush right foot to left foot

STEP 3

Man Step to the side and slightly back left foot

Lady Step forward right foot, diagonally

Weave

The Weave commences from Promenade Position facing diagonally to the centre, ending either in the Promenade Position or closed position – whichever the man decides to lead.

STEP 1

Man Step forward right foot, in Promenade Position

STEP 2

Man Step forward left foot, turning left

STEP 3

Man Step to the side and slightly backwards right foot, turning left

Lady Step forward left foot, in Promenade Position

Lady Step to the side and slightly backwards right foot, turning left

Lady Step to the side and slightly forward left foot, turning left

The Waltz

STEP 4

Man Step backwards left foot, outside partner

STEP 5

Man Step backwards right foot

STEP 6

Man Step to the side left foot in Promenade Position

Lady Step forward right foot, outside partner

Lady Step forward left foot

Lady Step to the side right foot, in Promenade Position

Weave (feet only)

The Weave feet positions, showing both the Promenade ending and the Closed ending

STEP 1

Man Step forward right foot, in Promenade Position
Lady Step forward left foot, in Promenade Position

STEP 2

Man Step forward left foot, turning left
Lady Step to the side and slightly backwards right foot, turning left

STEP 3

Man Step to the side and slightly backwards right foot, turning left
Lady Step to the side and slightly forward left foot, turning left

The Waltz

STEP 4

Man Step backwards left foot, outside partner
Lady Step forward right foot

STEP 5

Man Step backwards right foot
Lady Step to the side left foot, still turning to the left

STEP 6A Promenade end

Man Step to the side left foot, in Promenade Position
Lady Step to the side right foot, in Promenade Position

STEP 6B Closed end

Man Step to the side and slightly forward left foot, turning left
Lady Step to the side and slightly backwards right foot, turning left

Quickstep

The Quickstep is fabulous, darling. It is one of the most popular Ballroom dances because of its speed and splendour. You can break down the dance into two parts – the big sweeping movements across the floor and the jumps, hops, tricks and quick steps, which make the dance so exciting and fun to do. It is Erin's favourite dance (probably because she dances it with me!), I'm a bit of a mad quickstepper – all hell breaks loose, in a slightly controlled way. I love the sense of abandonment … in a tail suit.

The Quickstep is a dance that gives you a great sense of elation and, danced well, you feel swept away. It's like you're flying and it can literally take your breath away. I once danced Quickstep in a huge competition. We had made the final and the Quickstep was the last dance. I was feeling tired and emotional and then the music struck up and it was a real favourite of mine and the tune just lifted me. I flew around the floor, spinning, running, skipping, jumping, kicking – it was incredible – I was carried through on a wave of ecstasy and delight. And that is how the Quickstep should make you feel. It's tricky and intricate but the big movements of swishing and spinning across the floor take you away. I love that about it. The Quickstep was born out of the Foxtrot and they are my two favourite dances. When you dance, you think of energy,

vibrancy, excitement and emotion – these words epitomise the Quickstep. It has all the physical components to make you slump down into your chair at the end of it and say, 'that was amazing'. It's a dance you lose yourself in, which makes it so much fun to do. You are always pushing the boundaries of how far you can go without being out of control – you want that feeling of a controlled out of control, if that makes any sense!

The only problem of feeling like you're on a rollercoaster, in the same way a child looks at fireworks, is the anticipation of what is coming next – in the Quickstep you've got to keep your mind in tune so you know what step you are going to do to add that extra something. I am always trying to do a more exciting move, add a new layer, sweeping and turning and kicking and skipping and flying and spinning, but, I'm afraid it's not as easy as it sounds. You have to start from the beginning. As lovely as it is to fly you've got to start on the ground and get your speed up. And sometimes this can take a bit of time. A classic example of what the poet Anton once said, 'You're going to have to learn to walk before you can give it the full bifta!'.

Moving slowly with your partner is tricky enough, but moving quickly with your partner is a whole new galaxy of tricky-ness. Alas, it's one of those boring moments when you really have to learn your steps and take it slowly. The main issue of dancing at speed is trust and you need to build the trust between you and your partner. You've got to dance together and be spatially aware. Once again we come back to having perfect posture – a familiar phrase in the world of Anton Dancing. You don't want to kick your partner half to death, unless his last dance was rubbish and this is payback time!

The rhythm of the Quickstep is slow, quick-quick, slow. We will talk more about the music later. Now, I'm going to give you a little exercise that's going to be very simple. Of course when I say simple, what I mean is once you can do it perfectly, then it's simple. You're going to get the rhythm right yourself, and in harmony with your partner. The key to this is to dance the exercise confidently and in a positive fashion; dance this tentatively and you're going to get hurt, you'll be on the wrong foot and it just won't work – it will all be very disappointing to everybody concerned and fellas, the ladies will adjourn to the powder room to moan about your Quickstep. Being tentative has no place in the Quickstep – stand tall and walk strong.

So, assume the ballroom position of standing in front of your partner with perfect posture. Gentlemen, offer the lady a fabulous bodyline which she can dance with, present a good ribcage which she can place her body against; by doing this she will be fully aware of your weight

transference. Men, gather in your ladies, with a right front to right front position and take her in your normal Ballroom hold (man's right hand just under the lady's left shoulder blade, lady's left hand on the man's right arm, on his right bicep and men pick lady's right hand up in your left hand) making sure you give her a good frame, picking your elbows up so she knows you mean Quickstep action. Men, stand facing the wall at the top of the room as you are going to move down the room (obviously with the lady backing the wall). Men step forward with your right foot leading on a strong heel (ladies step back on your left foot) – this is just a normal walking step – on the slow count. Men step your left foot to the side, ladies step your right foot to the side, quick count, completely transferring your weight. Chaps, close right foot to left foot, ladies close left foot to right foot on quick count, once more, you've got it, change your weight. Then boys, step to the side with your left foot, girls with your right foot, for the final slow.

Now, repeat that all over again but the boys start off going backwards on the right foot and the ladies go forward on the left foot. So then men step to the side on your left foot (ladies step to the side on your right foot), then close up the feet (men right foot to left foot, ladies left foot to right). Boys now step to the side with your left foot and ladies with your right foot for the final slow. Now, we are going to repeat from the beginning, but with one slight difference – that the man now steps forward with his right foot but outside his partner: because of the speed of the music he cannot step inline. Now I hear you asking, 'what does outside his partner mean?' I hear your cries and pain.

Quickstep

Step forward on your right foot to the right of the lady's right foot – that's called 'outside of partner'; if I had stepped to the left of her right foot then that would have been 'in line'. If you try to step in line at speed you will kick the lady so step outside and stay happy. Continue this exercise always remembering to maintain your posture, stand tall and keep a good frame. And boys whenever you step forward from this point, step outside your partner. We talk about flow a lot in Ballroom dancing, it's a major component, and this exercise is designed to keep the fluidity of the dance. You've got to master this exercise as though you are flowing across the floor on a cushion of air, without any jerks and bumps; you should get a lovely sense of Quickstep with the body weights moving across the floor – freedom and fluidity – lovely. You don't need to accelerate you just need to let it go … and flow.

Ginger Rogers and Fred Astaire in The Story of Vernon and Irene Castle

I'm going to talk to you about rise and fall. We spoke about this in the Waltz briefly. I'm sorry to get technical on you but like all things, to develop this you must add a new layer, and this is the next layer after your perfect posture and correct hold (I appreciate I might be presuming a bit here but I have great confidence in all of you!). Now comes the step pattern, the rise and fall. As with the Waltz, boys you start forward on the heel, ladies normal backward walking step please. Now you step to the side (boys left foot, girls right foot), going directly to the toe. Join your feet together on toes, and then as you step to the side again for the last slow, onto a toe but directly lower onto the flat foot. Think the 'sl' part of the slow is the toe and the 'ow' part is the foot flat, ready to commence the whole exercise again with the girl coming forward and boy going back. This may seem all a bit tricky but it's this footwork that enables you to get that all–essential fluidity that we talked about earlier. Think of the footwork as the wheels of your beautiful running Rolls Royce or, if you're a bit quicker, something a little more sporty.

The timing of the Quickstep is 4/4 time and the tempo is 50 bars per minute so you can see it's pretty quick. Great Quickstep tunes are 'Sing Sing Sing' by Benny Goodman or something more modern would be 'Suddenly I See' by Katie Tunstall.

Quarter turn

The Quarter Turn is an important figure.
The starting figure of the Quickstep is
facing diagonally to the wall.

STEP 1

Man Step forward right foot,
turning right

Lady Step backward left foot,
turning right

STEP 2

Man Step to the side left
foot, continue turning

Lady Step to the side right foot

Quickstep

Ideas for a basic dance sequence

Quarter Turn, Progressive Chassé, Lock Step, Spin Turn,
Progressive Chassé

STEP 3

Man Close right foot to left
foot

STEP 4

Man Step to the side left
foot

Lady Close left foot to right foot

Lady Step diagonally forward
right foot

Chassé to the right

Chassé to the Right commences facing diagonally to the centre, and can be followed by a Back Lock

STEP 1

Man Step forward left foot

Lady Step backwards right foot

STEP 2

Man Step to the side right foot

Lady Step to the side left foot

Quickstep

STEP 3

Man Close left foot to right foot

STEP 4

Man Step to the side right foot

Lady Close right foot to left foot

Lady Step diagonally forward left foot

Lock step

This step is normally danced diagonally to the wall. It can be danced forward or backwards for the lady and man.

STEP 1

Man Step forward right foot, outside partner

STEP 2

Man Step diagonally forward left foot

Lady Step backwards left foot, partner outside

Lady Step backwards right foot

Quickstep

STEP 3

Man Cross right foot behind left foot

Lady Cross left foot in front of right foot

STEP 4

Man Step diagonally forward left foot

Lady Step diagonally backwards right foot

Lock step (feet only)

STEP 1

Man Step forward right foot, outside partner

Lady Step backwards left foot, partner outside

STEP 2

Man Step diagonally forward left foot

Lady Step backwards right foot

Quickstep

STEP 3

Man Cross right foot behind
left foot

Lady Cross left foot in front of
right foot

STEP 4

Man Step diagonally forward
left foot

Lady Step diagonally backwards
right foot

Natural spin turn

This step commences facing diagonally to wall and has a pivoting action for both man and lady, with the lady also doing a brush step.

STEP 1

Man Step forward right foot, turning right

STEP 2

Man Step to the side left foot, still turning

STEP 3

Man Close right foot to left foot

Lady Step backwards left foot, turning right

Lady Step to the side right foot

Lady Close left foot to right foot

Quickstep

STEP 4

Man Step backwards left foot, pivoting on it to the right (keeping the right foot in front of you)

STEP 5

Man Step forward right foot, still turning

STEP 6

Man Take a small step backwards and to the side left foot

Lady Step forward right foot, pivoting on it to the right

Lady Step backwards left foot, brush right foot to left foot

Lady Having brushed right foot to left foot, step diagonally forward on to it

Spin turn

The Spin Turn commences facing diagonally to the wall and can be danced at the corner of the room. There is a lovely feel of pivoting on steps 4 and 5.

STEP 1

Man Step forward right foot, turning right
Lady Step backwards left foot, turning right

STEP 2

Man Step to the side left foot, still turning
Lady Step to the side right foot

STEP 3

Man Close right foot to left foot
Lady Close left foot to right foot

Quickstep

STEP 4

Man Step backwards left foot, pivoting on it to right foot (keeping the right foot in front of you)
Lady Step forward right foot, pivoting on it to the right

STEP 5

Man Step forward right foot, still turning
Lady Step backwards left foot, brush right foot to left foot

STEP 6

Man Take a small step backwards and to the side left foot
Lady Having brushed right foot to left foot, step diagonally forward on to it.

Running finish

The Running Finish is normally preceded by a Back Lock and is danced down the line of dance.

STEP 1

Man Step backwards left foot, turning right, partner outside

STEP 2

Man Step to the side right foot, still turning

Lady Step forward right foot, turning right, outside partner

Lady Step to the side left foot, still turning

Quickstep

STEP 3

Man Step forward left foot, still turning

STEP 4

Man Step forward right foot, outside partner

Lady Step backwards right foot, still turning

Lady Step backward left foot, partner outside

Quick open reverse

The Quick Open Reverse is a left turning variation and commences facing diagonally to the centre. It is usually followed by a Chassé.

STEP 1

Man Step forward left foot, turning left

Lady Step backwards right foot, turning left

Quickstep

STEP 2

Man Step to the side right foot, still turning

Lady Step to the side left foot

STEP 3

Man Step backwards left foot, partner outside

Lady Step forward right foot, outside partner

Cha Cha Cha

The first dance I teach anyone who wants to learn a Latin American dance is the Cha Cha Cha. It really is a fun dance, with such lively music and a quicker tempo. It's one of those dances that gives you a great uplifting feeling inside. You'll also discover that it has a melting pot of styles and rhythms, all going on at the same time – which gives a great sense of freedom. But, most importantly, with the Cha Cha Cha you feel as if you are dancing from the moment you begin to learn it, rather than simply reciting the steps.

Personally, I like to be a bit mischievous when teaching this dance. I'll explain more about the timing in a moment but, because of the way that the timing works, it is a great dance to play around with and perhaps move shoulders or hips instead of taking a step. Isn't it great to get to do something with your body that you wouldn't normally do – all in the good name of dancing?

So you know that feeling when the radio's on at home and a great song comes on and so you start dancing around the kitchen because no one's looking? Well, with the Cha Cha Cha it's exactly the same sense of vibrant gay abandon! Oh – just make sure that your window cleaner doesn't catch you! As that old Irish proverb says, 'Work like you don't need money, Love like you've never been hurt, And dance like no one's watching'. Let's get you started then.

Stand facing each other without touching. Your hands should be in a double hand hold – which means that you're holding each others hands – with the palms facing your partner, not the floor or ceiling.

The man stands with the weight on his right foot and his left foot – the free leg – out to the side. Ladies, you have your weight on your left foot and your free foot is out to the side – mirroring your partner. We are starting this on the second beat in the bar – not the first – this begins on the two count. So for this beat, I'd like you to close your free foot to the foot you're standing on and transfer the weight over. So boys you're then standing with the weight on your left and the ladies have their weight on their right foot (your feet are still next to each other). Now, for beat three, you simply transfer your weight back over again to the original foot (boys, left and girls, right). For the fourth beat, boys will step to the side with their left foot and transfer weight to that left foot. Leave your right where it was, without weight on it. Girls, you're mirroring your partner by stepping to the side with your right foot and

transferring your weight and both of you need to remember to transfer your weight completely. Now I'd like you to close your feet again – that's boys bringing your right foot to the left and girls bringing your left foot to the right. This is the 'and' count (Think: two, three, four AND one, two, three, four etc) before going back into beat one. For beat one, the boys step to the side with their left foot, and girls step to the side with their right and once again both of you need to remember to transfer your weight over completely.

Now, I promised earlier that I'd explain how the timing works for this dance and, although we've just touched on it, brace yourself now for the technical bit! The timing for this dance starts on the second beat of the bar. So we begin on the two count of a one-two-three-four timing. The dance has a complete beat for two, and a complete beat for three, but the fourth beat is actually two half beats. That's why it becomes the 'and' that I spoke of earlier. So it's actually two-three-four and-one-two-three-four-and etc. It might make more sense if you think of it in this way two-three-CHA CHA CHA. two-three-CHA-CHA-CHA. The Cha Cha Cha part is the four and one part of the timing. It's actually how the dance got its name – the ladies' shoes would make that cha cha cha noise on the floor when dancing those beats. I do believe that makes the dance onomatopoeic! Good word, eh? That's the technical bit over, it wasn't too exhausting was it?

Now the point of this exercise is to get a real feeling of the rhythm of the dance being *the* single most important thing about it. Also, while you're doing this exercise with your partner, you will get to feel that changing of weight between you and this will help you to stay in harmony, a really key part of dancing with a partner. Despite the fact that your bodies aren't touching, just your hands, it's essential that you're moving together. This exercise will give you an opportunity to concentrate on the transfer of weight in the dance, without overwhelming yourself early on with steps and choreography.

One of the biggest problems with this dance is finding yourself on the wrong foot. This usually isn't because you've done a wrong step, as you might expect, but actually can often be because you've changed the rhythm. So you could have left a step out and ended up with your weight on the wrong foot. Or perhaps you've not transferred your weight correctly. If you can do the right rhythm and transfer your weight properly, then you'll always be on the correct foot. I've included this exercise – which I show everybody that I teach first off – because it's designed to get you to change weight properly, keep rhythm and attain harmony with your partner.

There's such an eclectic array of songs which suit this dance. It has a 4/4 rhythm (four beats per bar, regardless of us starting on the second beat) – with a quicker tempo than the Rumba. You could try Basement Jaxx's 'Red Alert' or 'Bingo Bango', or 'Sway' by Michael Buble.

PROD. MIER Y BROOKS, S. A.
presentan a
ANA BERTHA LEPE
en
¡QUÉ LINDO CHA CHA CHA!
con
JOSE VENEGAS
FERNANDO CASANOVA
ANDRES SOLER
Director GILBERTO MARTINEZ SOLARES ⋆ Dist. por DISTRIBUIDORA INDEPENDIENTE, S. A.

Forward basic

Forward and Back Basic is the beginning of the Cha Cha Cha and from here everything else follows.

STEP 1

Man Step forward left foot

Lady Step backwards right foot

STEP 2

Man Replace weight onto right foot

Lady Replace weight onto left foot

1950 *Que Lindo Cha Cha Cha!* movie poster

Cha Cha Cha

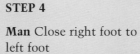

Ideas for a basic dance sequence

Forward and Back Basic, New York × 3, Spot Turn, Hand to Hand, Spot Turn

STEP 3

Man Step to the side left foot

STEP 4

Man Close right foot to left foot

STEP 5

Man Step to the side left foot

Lady Step to the side right foot

Lady Close left foot to right foot

Lady Step to the side right foot

Back basic

STEP 1

Man Step backwards
right foot

STEP 2

Man Replace weight onto
left foot

Lady Step forward left foot

Lady Replace weight onto
right foot

Cha Cha Cha

STEP 3

Man Step to the side
right foot

STEP 4

Man Close left foot to
right foot

STEP 5

Man Step to the side
right foot

Lady Step to the side
left foot

Lady Close right foot to
left foot

Lady Step to the side
left foot

New York

The New York can be danced both to the left and to the right.
It is preceded by the Forward and Back Basic.

STEP 1

Man Step forward left foot in
the left side position

STEP 2

Man Replace weight onto
right foot

Lady Step forward right foot in
the left side position

Lady Replace weight onto
left foot

Cha Cha Cha

STEP 3

Man Step to the side left foot, facing your partner

STEP 4

Man Close right foot to left foot

STEP 5

Man Step to the side left foot

Lady Step to the side right foot, facing your partner

Lady Close left foot to right foot

Lady Step to the side right foot

Hand to hand

The Hand to Hand can be danced both to the left and to the right and can be preceded by a Forward and Back Basic or a Spot Turn.

STEP 1

Man Step backwards right foot, in the left side position

STEP 2

Man Replace weight onto left foot

Lady Step backwards on the left foot, in the left side position

Lady Replace weight onto right foot

Cha Cha Cha

STEP 3

Man Step to the side
right foot, facing
your partner

STEP 4

Man Close left foot
to right foot

STEP 5

Man Step to the side
right foot

Lady Step to the side
left foot, facing your
partner

Lady Close right foot
to left foot

Lady Step to the side
left foot

Basic to fan

The Basic to Fan is followed by the Hockey Stick or the Alemana.

STEP 1

Man Step forward left foot
Lady Step backwards right foot

STEP 2

Man Replace weight right foot
Lady Replace weight left foot

STEP 3

Man Step to the side left foot
Lady Step to the side right foot

STEP 4

Man Close right foot to left foot
Lady Close left foot to right foot

Cha Cha Cha

STEP 5

Man Step to the side left foot
Lady Step to the side right foot

STEP 6

Man Step backwards right foot
Lady Step forward left foot

STEP 7

Man Replace weight left foot
Lady Step to the side and slightly backwards right foot

STEP 8

Man Step to the side right foot
Lady Step backwards left foot

STEP 9

Man Close left foot to right foot
Lady Cross right foot in front of left foot

STEP 10

Man Step to the side right foot
Lady Step backwards left foot

Hockey stick from fan

STEP 1

Man Step forward left foot
Lady Close right foot to left foot

STEP 2

Man Replace weight onto right foot
Lady Step forward left foot

In this figure, when the lady turns left, the man must not be too far away from her, so keep close and don't lose contact!

STEP 3

Man Small step to the side left foot
Lady Step forward right foot

STEP 4

Man Close right foot to left foot
Lady Cross left foot behind right foot

Cha Cha Cha

STEP 5

Man Step to the side left foot
Lady Step forward right foot

STEP 6

Man Place right foot behind left foot in a small step
Lady Step forward left foot

STEP 7

Man Step forward left foot
Lady Step forward right foot, turn to the left and face your partner

STEP 8

Man Step forward right foot
Lady Step backwards left foot

STEP 9

Man Cross left foot behind right foot
Lady Cross right foot in front of left foot

STEP 10

Man Step forward right foot
Lady Step backwards left foot

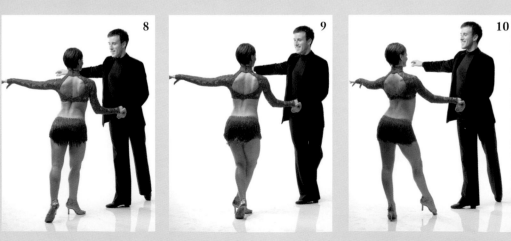

Alemana from fan

STEP 1

Man Step forward left foot
Lady Close right foot to left foot

STEP 2

Man Replace weight onto right foot
Lady Step forward left foot

This is a turn to the right for the lady. You will find this is much easier if you take the 5th step of the Fan (lady's right foot stepping forward) towards the man.

STEP 3

Man Take a small step to the side left foot
Lady Step forward right foot

STEP 4

Man Close left foot to right foot
Lady Cross left foot behind right foot

Cha Cha Cha

STEP 5

Man Step to the side left foot
Lady Step forward right foot, starting to turn right

STEP 6

Man Step backwards right foot
Lady Turning to the right, step forward left foot under the arm to the man's left side

STEP 7

Man Replace weight onto left foot
Lady Continuing to turn right, step forward right foot away from your partner

STEP 8

Man Take a small step to the side right foot
Lady Step to the side left foot, turning to face your partner

STEP 9

Man Close left foot to right foot
Lady Close right foot to left foot

STEP 10

Man Step to the side right foot
Lady Step to the side left foot

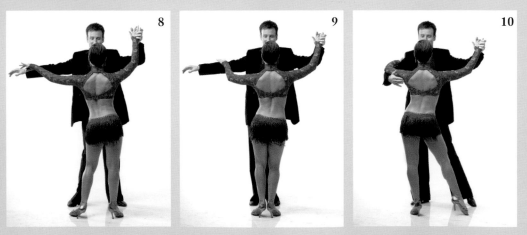

Spot turn

The Spot Turn can be danced to the left or to the right, preceded by the New York or the Hand to Hand.

STEP 1

Man Step forward left foot in left side position, then turn right to end with right foot in front

STEP 2

Man Replace weight onto right foot

Lady Step forward right foot in left side position, then turn left to end with left foot in front

Lady Replace weight onto left foot

Cha Cha Cha

STEP 3

Man Step to the side left foot to face your partner

STEP 4

Man Close right foot to left foot

STEP 5

Man Step to the side left foot

Lady Step to the side right foot to face your partner

Lady Close left foot to right foot

Lady Step to the side right foot

Backward lock step (feet only)

The Lock Step must be danced with the heel of the back foot staying off the floor during the lock section (the crossing section). The three steps of the Lock are used as the cha cha cha when travelling forward and backwards, so when you move to the side it's a Chassé and when you move backwards it's a Lock.

STEP 1

Man Step forward left foot
Lady Step backwards right foot

STEP 2

Man Replace weight onto right foot
Lady Replace weight onto left foot

STEP 3

Man Step backwards left foot
Lady Step forward right foot

STEP 4

Man Cross right foot in front of left foot
Lady Cross left foot behind right foot

STEP 5

Man Step backwards left foot
Lady Step forward right foot

Forward lock step (feet only)

STEP 1

Man Step backwards right foot
Lady Step forward left foot

STEP 2

Man Replace weight onto left foot
Lady Replace weight onto right foot

STEP 3

Man Step forward right foot
Lady Step backwards left foot

STEP 4

Man Cross left foot behind right foot
Lady Cross right foot in front of left foot

STEP 5

Man Step forward right foot
Lady Step backwards left foot

Forward and back basic

This is just a reminder of the foot pattern for the Forward Basic for the man and the Back Basic for the woman. A simple step but so important and, as ever, don't forget to change weight!

STEP 1

Man Step forward left foot
Lady Step backwards right foot

STEP 2

Man Replace weight onto right foot
Lady Replace weight onto left foot

Cha Cha Cha

STEP 3

Man Step to the side
left foot
Lady Step to the side
right foot

STEP 4

Man Close right foot to
left foot
Lady Close left foot to
right foot

STEP 5

Man Step to the side
left foot
Lady Step to the side
right foot

The Jive

The Jive is the newest of all the dances to become one of the standardised Latin American dances. Because this dance came out of the social climate of the Second World War, when the guys and girls didn't know when they would next get to dance together, it was celebrated as a fabulous new frenzied style of dancing, where almost anything went. It became a huge release and escape and you were taken away to another place and time. That's what's great about it. I love the fact that a dance can transport you to another world. It's amazing to think a dance can take you away from the horrors in your life and for a few short moments your spirit can be lifted and re-energised. That's what dancing in general is all about for me. Obviously I wasn't around at that time but I do know that dancing can re-invigorate the soul. It's an excuse to let your hair down and I'm glad that it was a dance that enabled them to do exactly that. All dances have this capacity and they can be seen as a reflection of the social climate of their time. For some reason the Jive seems to have a bigger impact, I suppose because it's the newest and most poignant; it affected the whole world. Like all dances it develops and evolves, and so it isn't the same as the one danced at that time, but it still has that sense of escapism.

I love dances that have a bit of a story or a reason for dancing them. Whether I choreograph a story into them or there is a story that underpins the dance, this is what motivates me. In the Jive, I try to use the chorcography to show that freedom of expression, the sense of throwing your legs about and letting go, which is so inherent in the dance. It has many elements – lindy hop, rock'n'roll, swing, jitterbug – which makes it a lively high tempo dance, with the feeling that 'anything goes', but you have to maintain a level of technique otherwise it gets messy … and a bit dangerous. We don't have any of the high lifts of the pure rock'n'roll dances in Jive – it's actually an illegal manoeuvre – so we tend to keep it strictly on the floor.

We're going to start gently on this one, as I think it's probably the wise way to go. We don't want a groin strain or a hamstring injury before you even get going. I've got two little exercises that are almost the same thing, one very gentle and the other a little more upbeat. So we're going to start off with the slower one, to get you into it because I know what you're like, you boys, you get all excited and rush into it and throw your partner around because you think you know how to do it because you saw Auntie Ethel and Uncle Norman doing it at their Golden

Wedding before he put her hip out as he swung her round and she remembered why she'd given up the Jive in the sixties and took up gardening instead. So here we go. Stand in front of your partner facing each other, with a slight gap between you but hold hands (boys, with your right hand take the girl's left hand and take her right hand with your left hand, i.e. a double hand hold). This little exercise is on the spot, so you're not actually moving anywhere, just rocking from side to side. So, boys step to the left with your left foot, girls step to the right with your right foot. Boys then step to the side with your right foot, girls step to the side with your left foot, making sure you change weight (oh, sounds so familiar doesn't it?), so in effect boys you rock left and then right and girls you do the opposite. Then we do a Back Rock – boys step back on your left foot, girls step back on your right foot and then boys rock forward onto your right foot and girls on your left foot, obviously changing weight.

Now repeat again, side, side, back rock, side, side, back rock. The rhythm is slow, slow, quick-quick. Okay, that's the gentle one. You see, that wasn't too exhausting was it? Now we are going to do the same exercise but slightly quicker and with a little extra. Rather than just rock to the side we are going to do a little Chassé. Now that consists of this: boys, starting with your left foot, do a step to the side but don't make it too big because you will just look a twit. So with your left foot moving to your left, close your right foot to the left foot and then step to the side again with your left foot. Girls do the natural opposite starting with your right foot. Then we come back. Boys, starting with your right

foot, so that will be side, close, side. Go to the side then close with your left foot and then step to the side again with your right foot. Then boys, with your left foot, and girls with your right foot, do your Back Rock. The rhythm to this is slow, quick quick, slow, quick quick, quick quick. When I say slow, it's all relative, it isn't that slow, the quick quick should add up to one slow. That's called a Jive Chassé. That's an integral part of the Jive. This has got to be lively, bright and FUN. You don't want to do this on flat feet, you need a bit of bounce in the knees, without going mad obviously.

The point of this exercise is twofold; firstly it's the importance of learning the Back Rock which is crucial to the dance. You could almost stand still for the rest of the dance and, as long as the Back Rock is correct you will remain on the right foot and in the right time. And the second is harmony, because when you develop the dance and the boys twirl the girls under their arms, boys, you will understand the importance of dancing together. If you're in time with each other then the man can lead the lady into another part of the dance with ease and style – because that's what we're looking for – ease and style.

The problems really are keeping in time, not missing the beat and once again we must address the doom that is not transferring weight. How it keeps me up at night, 'woe is me and thrice woe', it's just so lamentable.

The music is 2/4 but you can use 4/4 music – I know it's not right, I can hear you telling me off, but you can use it, it's fine. A classic oldie is Jerry Lewis's 'Great Balls of Fire'.

The chassé

The Jive Chassé can be danced to the side, forward, backwards or turning and is an integral part of the Jive rhythm.

STEP 1

Man Take a small step to the side left foot

Lady Take a small step to the side right foot

STEP 2

Man Close right foot to left foot

Lady Close left foot to right foot

STEP 3

Man Take a small step to the side left foot

Lady Take a small step to the side right foot

Jive

> ### *Ideas for a basic dance sequence*
> *Basic Jive Chassé to the left, then to the right, Back Rock, Change of Place*
> *Right to Left, Back Rock, Change of Place Left to Right, Back Rock, Change*
> *the Hand Behind the Back, Back Rock, Change the Hand again, Change*
> *of Place Left to Right, American Spin*

STEP 4

Man Take a small step
to the side right foot

STEP 5

Man Close left foot
to right foot

STEP 6

Man Take a small step
to the side right foot

Lady Take a small step
to the side left foot

Lady Close right foot
to left foot

Lady Take a small step
to the side left foot

Back rock

The Back Rock is normally danced at the beginning and end of every figure.

STEP 1

Man Step backwards left foot
Lady Step backwards right foot

Jive

STEP 2

Man Replace weight
onto right foot
Lady Replace weight
onto left foot

Change of place, left to right

The Change of Place can be danced left to right and right to left. Both commence and end with the Back Rock.

STEP 1

Man Take a small step to the side left foot
Lady Take a small step to the side right foot

STEP 2

Man Close right foot to left foot
Lady Close left foot to right foot

STEP 3

Man Take a small step to the side left foot
Lady Take a small step to the side right foot, starting to turn

STEP 4

Man Step to the side right foot
Lady Step to the side, while turning right, left foot

STEP 5

Man Close left foot to right foot
Lady Close right foot to left foot, turning right

Jive

STEP 6

Man Facing your partner; take a small side step right foot
Lady Facing your partner; take a side step left foot

STEPS 7 & 8

Man The Back Rock
Lady The Back Rock

Change of place, right to left

STEP 1

Man Step backwards
left foot
Lady Step backwards
right foot

STEP 2

Man Replace weight onto
right foot
Lady Replace weight onto
left foot

STEP 3

Man Take a small step to
the side left foot
Lady Take a small step
to the side right foot,
turning left

STEP 4

Man Close right foot to
left foot
Lady Close left foot to
right foot, still turning

Jive

Commence in Open Position with the lady turning to the left. Start and end with a Back Rock.

STEP 5

Man Take a small step to the side left foot
Lady Take a small step to the side right foot, turning to face partner

STEP 6

Man Take a small step to the side right foot
Lady Take a small step to the side left foot

STEP 7

Man Close left foot to right foot
Lady Close right foot to left foot

STEP 8

Man Take a small step to the side right foot
Lady Take a small step to the side left foot

American spin

The American Spin commences with a Back Rock, the spin for the lady is taken on step 3. Boys, don't forget to catch your partner after you've lead the spin!

STEP 1

Man Take a small step to the side left foot
Lady Take a small step to the side right foot

STEP 2

Man Close right foot to left foot
Lady Close left foot to right foot

STEP 3

Man Take a small step to the side left foot
Lady Step onto right foot and turn right to face partner

Jive

STEP 4

Man Take a small step to the side right foot
Lady Take a small step to the side left foot

STEP 5

Man Close left foot to right foot
Lady Close right foot to left foot

STEP 6

Man Take a small step to the side right foot
Lady Take a small step to the side left foot

Change the hand behind the back

STEP 1

Man With left foot, step towards your partner's right side
Lady With right foot, take a small step towards your partner's right side

STEP 2

Man Close right foot to left foot
Lady Close left foot to right foot

STEP 3

Man Step forward left foot, turning right
Lady Step forward right foot

$\mathcal{J}$ive

STEP 4

Man Step forward right foot, still turning so as you face your partner
Lady Step to the side left foot to face your partner

STEP 5

Man Close left foot to right foot
Lady Close right foot to left foot

STEP 6

Man Take a small step to the side right foot
Lady Take a small step to the side left foot

Stop and go (1)

The Stop and Go commences in an open hold and can be danced following the Change of Place, Left to Right

STEP 1

Man The back rock
Lady The back rock

STEP 2

Man The back rock
Lady The back rock

Jive

STEP 3

Man Step forward left foot
Lady Step forward right foot, turning left

STEP 4

Man Close right foot to left foot
Lady Close left foot to right foot, still turning

Stop and go (2)

STEP 5

Man Step forward left foot
Lady Step backwards right foot

STEP 6

Man Step forward right foot
Lady Step backwards left foot

STEP 7

Man Replace weight onto left foot
Lady Replace weight onto right foot

Jive

STEP 8

Man Take a small step to the side right foot
Lady Step forward left foot, turning right

STEP 9

Man Close left foot to right foot
Lady Close right foot to left foot, still turning

STEP 10

Man Take a small step to the side right foot
Lady Step back left foot to face your partner

Whip

The Whip is danced from an open hold and can be danced following the Change of Place, Left to Right or after the Change of Hand Behind the Back.

STEP 1

Man Cross right foot behind left foot

Lady With left foot step towards partner's right side

STEP 2

Man Step to the side left foot

Lady Step forward between your partner's feet right foot

Jive

STEP 3

Man Step to the side
right foot

STEP 4

Man Close left foot to
right foot

STEP 5

Man Step to the side
right foot

Lady Step to the side
left foot

Lady Close right foot to
left foot

Lady Step to the side
left foot

Whip (feet only)

Start and finish facing the Line of Direction, follow with the Three Step, Reverse Wave or, if at a corner, Change of Direction. Start and finish with a Back Rock.

STEP 1

Man Cross right foot behind left foot
Lady With left foot step towards partner's right side

STEP 2

Man Step to the side left foot
Lady Step forward between your partner's feet right foot

STEP 3

Man Step to the side
right foot
Lady Step to the side
left foot

STEP 4

Man Close left foot to
right foot
Lady Close right foot to
left foot

STEP 5

Man Step to the side
right foot
Lady Step to the side
left foot